AF322611

# SINUOUS

# HEART

## Fay van Burg

BUTTERDRAGONS
PUBLISHING

Title: Sinuous Heart

Author: Fay van Burg

Copyright © 2024 Butterdragons® Publishing

All Rights Reserved



Published by Butterdragons® Publishing

https://butterdragons.com

ISBN: 9789493287723 (ebook)

ISBN: 9789493287730 (hardback)

ISBN: 9789493287747 (audio book)

Cover Design by: Dazed Designs

Audio book narrated by Martha Webb

For my English teachers

What if you took a chance on me
What if you opened your heart to me
What if I could heal your pain
What if distance weren't a problem
What if we forgot about our past
What if we began anew, together
What if I were everything you need
What if we were perfect together…

Books help me escape my reality
A reality that is harsh
A reality that is cruel
A reality that is dark
A reality that is rough
Books take me away to another world
A world where I am free
A world where I am happy
A world where I can be
Me

The sun, the rain
The fire, the water
The soil, the wind
The earth, the air
The four elements
The four elements that our world consist of
The four elements that define our lives
That define us
The four elements that are a force of nature
Fire, volcanoes, trees burning
Water, floods, children drowning
Earth, sink holes, houses crumbling
Air, tornadoes, cars flying
These four elements can destroy us
These four elements can give us life
Fire gives us warmth when we're cold
Water gives us precious liquid to drink
Earth gives us food to eat
Air gives us oxygen to breathe
Respect nature
Respect our world, our planet Gaia
And her children
And the elements will protect us
Protect us against the wrath that Mother Nature
can bring
Or else Mother Nature's wrath will find you
Unyielding in Her fury

Stories in my head that won't get out
Ideas circling in my mind, unable to finalise
Writer's block hits hard
Fragmented ideas flowing through my mind
Sentences whispering
Words speaking
So many shards, and yet no cohesive story
Separate scenes that make no sense
So, I pick up a pen and write
Until words start making sense

What is beauty?
Is it being thin
Is it having perfect hair
Is it wearing perfect makeup
Is it wearing the prettiest clothes
What is beauty?
Is it being yourself
Is it being confident
Is it loving myself
Is it being comfortable in my own skin
What is beauty?
Is it defined by society
Or is it defined by me?

Zeus, God of thunder
Poseidon, God of the seas
Hades, God of the Underworld
These are my chosen Gods
Athena, Goddess of wisdom
Apollo, God of music
Aphrodite, Goddess of love
These are the Gods I worship
Demeter, Goddess of harvest
Artemis, Goddess of the hunt
Ares, God of war
It took me a while to find them
Hephaestus, God of blacksmiths
Hermes, God of messages
Dionysus, God of vines
I feel comfortable with them
Hera, Goddess of marriage
Nemesis, Goddess of revenge
Pan, God of the wild
I don't want to leave them
Persephone, Goddess of spring
Nike, Goddess of victory
Fortuna, Goddess of fortune
I feel happy with them
They accept me as I am

Physical pain, mental pain
Both so alike, but different
Physical hurt for everyone to see
Mental hurt unseen by all
One can be described and mostly healed
But how can you heal from something
indescribable?
Stab of pain telling us
Something is wrong with the body
But pain of the mind shuts down the body
Why does it have to be that way?
And once the pain is gone, we've grown
So, in order to grow
We somehow need to endure all this pain
To become a stronger person better than before

Why can't you just f*cking listen to me?
Am I speaking in a language you don't
understand?
You promised you would try, but you never
did
You still don't understand
All you can do is scream
I'm always in the wrong
You can only ever point out my flaws
And you never say you are proud of me
All I can feel from you is disdain
I want respect and understanding from you
I deserve it for how hard I try
So maybe, you could try harder, too

I've got one foot in the cradle
And one in the grave
I'm no longer a child
But not an adult either
Something in between
Old enough to make my own decisions
But not old enough to live on my own
Old enough to pay my own bills
But not old enough for a well-paid job
I feel mature and yet
I feel like mommy's little girl
Sometimes, I feel I can conquer the world
But other times, I feel powerless
I guess this is what becoming an adult feels
like

Spells and magic and candles
Herbs and crystals and incense
Pentagrams to protect against evil
Healing through shadow work
Meditate to calmness
Honour your ancestors
Burn what needs to be left behind
Plant what needs to grow
Be whole as yourself
Feel the power within your soul
You are the granddaughter of great women
You carry their souls
You are powerful
You carry a fire inside
You are the force they didn't expect
You are a woman
You are Nature

Pain that is unseen
Illness that is invisible
Do too much, pain will come
Do too little, pain will come anyway
Invisible flames, licking my shoulder
Invisible needles, pricking my legs
Some days are bearable
Some days are not
Never knowing if I went too far
Until I wake up in pain the next morning
Pain that is unseen
Illness that is invisible

Sometimes, I think my soul mate is in another universe
Because I can't seem to find him here
I like to think he got stuck
Waiting for some evil sorcerer to free him
And let him come to me
Sometimes, I think my soul mate only exists on the silver screen
Or within the pages of a novel
Maybe I will never find him
But maybe I will, someday

I read
Because it helps me escape
This monotonous life
I want sword fights
And dragons and gold
I want adventure
And romance and mystery
I want magic
And spells and potions
I want horror
And blood and gore
I write
Because it helps me process my feelings
My unspoken inner thoughts
I need rage
And anger and fury
I need sadness
And melancholy and cries
I need fear
And guilt and pain
Books and pens are my best friends
Always there for me
Never judging

I am falling apart
Into a million little pieces
Some are too small, too sharp
Some are bigger, less dangerous
But painful nonetheless
I try to pick up the pieces
They cut into my hands
Blood is dripping onto the floor
With the red of my blood
My pain is flowing away
As the blood dries, the wounds heal
And once the splatter is cleaned off the floor
I start feeling okay again

When the leaves start falling
It is the time for candles
And blankets and spells
When the moon shines bright
In the pitch-black night
It is the time for hot tea and books
Autumn has arrived
And I feel alive once more

I wish you find someone who will be good to
you
Someone who will never misuse your
weakness
Or make fun of you
I wish you find someone who will try to never
hurt you
I wish you find someone who will support you
It is not what you deserve but it is what you
need
To become a much better person than you are

This is how it feels to not belong
It's like being invisible
Like nobody sees you
It's like being on the outside, freezing
Looking through a window
Into a cozy room with a fireplace
Where everyone is having fun
And you are a pariah
That no one understands
They just keep you around
For convenience, in case they need you
Surrounded by people with no one to talk to
This is how it feels to not belong

Bats fluttering in the night sky
Creatures crawling in the dark
Shadows creeping in the corridors
Feral cats stalking the dark alleys
Beasts prowling the forest
Witches crafting under the moon
Entities lurking in the house
Leaves slowly falling down
Days growing darker and darker
This the season
Of witches, ghouls, and ghosts
This is the season
Of Halloween

When the clock creeps closer to midnight
And the world becomes quieter
When you hear the soft sounds of a sleeping
city
And my thoughts are still, for once
When the pavement smells like solitude and
calm
That's when I truly become alive
When the clock strikes twelve
I become truly awake

She has starlight in her eyes
And sunshine in her veins
She is pure happiness
And I envy her for that
I am darkness, and sorrow, and pain
And she misses those
So maybe, just maybe
We need each other for balance

When people cry
And tears fall from their eyes
They water themselves
Like they would water plants
To make them grow
Their tears are not shed in vain
They have a purpose
To release the pressure
To make them grow

My mind is a fortress
Wrapped in barbed wire
Unwilling to let anyone past it
My heart is a frozen wasteland
Too cold for anyone to survive in
My mind is a starless night
In which you are unable to see
With no promise of dawn
My heart refuses to let anyone in
Hurt one too many times
I would rather be alone
Before I hurt again

I feel your arms around me when I sleep
I feel you hold my hand when I am scared
I hear your loving whispers
I smell you on my pillow when I feel alone
You are always close to me
But I wake up alone
You are not here
You were never here
You were a dream
A figment of my imagination

When you feel alone
Hurt and angry
That everyone seems insignificant
And you push them away
Ignore them
Forgetting they are there
Stop yourself
Before you have no one left

She was there for me
In my darkest hour
She was there for me
When I felt utterly alone
She was there for me
In my rage-filled hurt
She was there for me
When I was happy
She was there for me
When I was dancing around in my room
She was there for me
When I didn't know what to say
She was there for me
She never went away
She is my summer sun
When no one understands me
Mother Nature does

I want to walk barefoot in the forest
Winter wind on my face, crisp and cold
Old leaves and dirt beneath my toes
My mind as clear as the night sky
My future as bright as the full moon
My love as infinite as the stars

Grief can be as gentle as a summer breeze
Grief can be as hard as a wrecking ball
Punching through a concrete wall
It can leave you shattered
Crumpled on the floor like a little child
Grief can physically hurt
Feeling your heart is being torn out
But grief can be hardly noticeable
And then suddenly hit you
Like a rock, hard and relentless
Grief means you loved
Grief is a reminder that love existed

Think positive thoughts
Meditate and be calm
Go with the flow
What you give, you get back
What a great advice that would be
If it weren't so f*cking difficult
When your mind is broken
And you can't find all the pieces

Mechanical, like a ticking clock
Red, like a drop of blood
Blue, like the summer sky
Yellow, like the daisies in the field
Green, like the spring grass
Orange, like the fall leaves
Hard, like the granite stone
Smooth, like marble
Precious, like a gemstone
Pure, like shining silver
White, like fresh snow
Black, like the darkest night
Long, like the road ahead
Colourful, like the rainbow
Fast, like a falling star
Tall, like a sturdy mountain
Deep, like the vast ocean
Loyal, like a sweet dog
Free, like a flying bird
Hot, like a burning flame
Shiny, like polished metal
Beautiful, like a love song
Mythical, like a mighty dragon
Enchanting, like a fairytale

I crave sunlight
I long for spring
I want to start over
Begin again
Be reborn
I want this depression to end
This is what happens
When the seasonal melancholy takes over
When Persephone returns to Hades
And I feel heavy once more
I can feel Demeter's grief
So, I wait out the time with her
Until her daughter finally returns
To the mortal world
And brings the sunshine with her
To chase away my clouds

I know you will protect me
Wherever I go
Whether I know you're there or not
Whether I ask you to or not
You will always safeguard me
You will always bring me happiness
Even in the most ridiculous ways you can
think of
However you show your face, I will recognize
you
And I want to thank you for that
Thank you for being there when I need you
But mainly, thank you for showing me there is
always joy to be found
If I look closely enough

I understand Atlas
For I too, carry the weight of the world on my
shoulders
In that, the old god and I are the same
Both carrying too much load for the strength
we were given
Nearly buckling under all the weight
But we endure, we stand, we keep going, we
suffer
We wait and wait and wait until there is
someone else
Strong enough, or stupid enough, to take the
burden from us
When we finally rest, we sleep
For days, weeks, months, years
Atlas and I aren't so different from one another
We both carry a load too heavy for us to bear

I am so done with your anger pain
That you always, always take out on me
You are toxic, incredibly toxic
And you like to blame it on me
And you get angry with me
And you wonder where I learned this type of
behaviour
While all I am is a mirror of you
But you are too afraid to face the mirror
So, we are stuck in an endless circle
But I will shatter it
I will be the one to end this generational
trauma
I will do what you couldn't
Watch me break this curse

When my anger symbolizes that I am never
understood
When my sadness symbolizes the loneliness I
feel
When my fear symbolizes the anxiety of being
abandoned
When my disgust symbolizes my immense
need to prove myself
But what does my happiness symbolize?

I follow you, wherever you go
But you never follow me
Standing in line, all alone
Because you left me, again
Crying at my favourite place
Because you hurt me, again
I finally realised, I'm at the bottom of your list
We are not equals in this relationship

I'm all by myself
After what you did
It was meticulous, calculated
And now I am sitting here
With a broken heart in my hands
Blood seeping through my fingers
Staining the ground bright red
Desperately trying to find something
To stop the bleeding
I understand now that some people
Only care about themselves
I can care for them all I want
But they won't to care for me
They'll keep letting me down
I guess that's why I need to walk away

I saw you struggling
So, I offered my help
But you yelled at me
As if I were there to hurt you
And that hurt me
I was simply trying to help
But this behaviour of yours
Stopped me in my tracks
And I won't try that again

Do you ever wish you can go back
To the days when life was simple
Uncomplicated, with not a care in the world
I want to go back that wonderland
I want to be a child again
I miss my childhood
The time when I made friends
As easy as breathing
The time when my only concern
Was being on time in school
When I didn't have to work so hard
For just a few cents
I want to go back to those days
But instead, I must move on

I made a mistake
And I owned it
I apologised
I told you I was wrong
But you wouldn't accept it
You were cruel
Your insults made me feel worthless
Made me want to leave
And quit what we had built
I wanted to disappear
I despise what you did
You hurt me and broke my trust
And left it crumpled on the floor like a piece of
paper
Tossed aside like it was worthless
And you broke my heart
You tore it out of my chest
And crushed it in the palm of your hand
Like it was nothing
I guess I should thank you
For showing me your true colours
And teaching me this lesson
Our friendship, a painful memory

My knives are sharpened
My mind is ready for battle
My pen is my sword
I will fight for what is mine
I have to be strong
And bend before I break
But I will no longer bow to your will
I'm done being pushed around
You don't always know best
There are others who know better
But you refuse to admit it
So, I'll keep fighting
Until my voice is heard

When thrill-seeking boys become thrill-
seeking men
Roaring engines and lightning-fast cars
Ready for it, for the big race
The lights go off and away they go
Twenty drivers, fighting for the title
Once the flag falls
One is crowned
The winner of all

The happy tunes fade away
And turn into something sinister
The wind is picking up and you see it
A mansion on top of a hill
Dark, bleak, ominous
Your hand glides over the wooden banister
As you wait to enter this haunted place
The menacing music gets louder
And the anticipation grows
Then, finally, it is your turn
So, you enter the mansion
Candlelight flickers, the air is still
Paintings stretch and reveal hidden secrets
Until you reach a hallway
With pictures changing
Or is it all in your mind?
You stop dead in your tracks
Once you see her and you hear him
Welcome to the manor!

I always cry thinking about this place
Happy if I am coming
Sad if I am leaving
Whenever I see the famous landmarks
I take a breath of relief
I feel like I've finally come home
And I hope that I can one day
Call this place my home
I want to go back whenever I leave
Because it feels more home than my home
does

I miss the girl I once was
I look in the mirror and I don't recognise
myself
I look into my eyes
And where I found happiness before
All I see now is sorrow and pain
I used to have a carefree life
Not worrying about a thing
But that little careless girl got lost
She vanished, disappeared somewhere
But I promise I will find her again

I used to be bullied
People called me weird and crazy
For I have passion for unconventional things
Things that made me who I am
And now they might read my poetry
And find me not so weird and crazy anymore
But nothing about me changed
I stayed true to myself

When people ask me
Why I refuse to medicate
Here is what I say
They make me hollow
They make me a shell
Of the person I am
They shut off my feelings
They shut off my thoughts
Including the good ones
That is why I don't medicate
Because it turns me into someone I don't want
to be
They rip the excitement for life out of my chest
That is why I don't medicate

Dear future husband,
Please be patient with me
I haven't done this before
When I get nervous
I start to chatter
I want date nights in our jammies
Snuggled on the couch
Or laying with my head in your lap
Reading my newest book
I want unexpected hugs
When I am making food
I want you to hold onto me and don't let go
Until I feel better
I want kisses in the rain and laughter
I want you to tell me all about your favourite
stuff
I want you to protect me
From all that tries to hurt me
I want you to take me as I am
I want you to allow me to be me
And love me the way I am
And my home will always be with you

If they hurt you, let them go
If they undervalue you, let them go
If they judge you, for being you
Don't stop being you, let them go
If they dull your shine, shine brighter
Your happiness matters more
Don't regret missing out on life
Just let them go

Do you know those moment
When everything changes
When all the what-ifs and would've, could've,
should've run through your head
Mourn what you lost
Let regrets be your lessons
Remember that you cannot change the past
But you can affect the future

Dear childhood bullies,
How does it feel to be immortalised in black
ink?
How does it feel to know I still suffer from
what you did?
Still, to this day, after all this time
But I suppose I should be grateful
Because I turned the pain into art
And I am healing
It is a beautiful place to be
Maybe you should try to heal yourself, too

My dear,
I am a poet
Treat me like glass
For I am fragile
Treat me like dynamite
For I am explosive
Treat me like fire
For I am hot
Treat me like ice
For I am cold
But most of all
Treat me like a tall tree
For I will not bow

I love how Athena
Stands behind me
Spear in hand
Ready to protect me
I love how Loki
Makes me laugh
Showing me chaos
When I am sad
I see Hades
Like a grumpy older brother
I love Aphrodite
So fiercely protective
And a little jealous
I love the ancient Gods
They are my family
They are my teachers
They are larger than life
And a part of me as a person
Until the day I join Hades

A butterfly can't see its own wings
And, darling, neither can you
But believe me when I say
You are breathtaking

If he won't, another one will
And sweetie, that is the truth
Don't settle, ever
If he cannot give you
All that you deserve
Love, respect, friendship
Pack up and leave
Find the one who will treat you right
The one who will treat you
Like the divine creature you are

Dear mother,
I am sorry we fight
I am sorry we argue
I am sorry I scream
And I'm sorry I don't always
Understand you
But I feel misunderstood, as well
I feel hurt, too
I don't like to argue with you
But I feel like I have to
I feel like it's the only way
I can make you understand me

When a shy girl
Gets courage
To do what she fears
When a shy girl
Asks a guy on a date
Without fearing rejection
When a shy girl
Starts singing in public
Along with the music
Not caring who hears
When a shy girl
Forgets about other people's opinions
And starts being her own self
That is called growth

Medusa wasn't a victim
She was a survivor
Athena didn't punish her
Instead, she protected her
From ever being touched
By another man
Who doesn't know
The meaning of the word
No

What if Persephone wasn't kidnapped?
But she went willingly with Hades
Because she craved the darkness
She craved the cold
But mostly, she craved being away
From her controlling mother
And she craved the love
Hades was giving her
What if she was everything but helpless?

Dear Athena,
Thank you, for teaching me
Wisdom, courage, and faith
Dear Hades,
Thank you, for teaching me
Protection, patience, and values
Dear Loki,
Thank you, for teaching me
Joy, peace, and clarity
Dear Aphrodite,
Thank you, for teaching me
Love, beauty, and self-worth
You are all my guides
Thank you, for teaching me
Thank you, for protecting me
My body and my mind
Thank you for being there
When I needed you most

I am not interested in someone
Who wants me for a fleeting moment
Just because I'm near
I want someone who chooses me
Intentionally and for a lifetime
To be his partner

I'm starting to understand
Why animals go into hibernation
Not because of the cold
I don't mind that, I am warm inside
But the hell these cold months
Put me through
I want to sleep until they pass
Wake me up
When Persephone leaves Hades
And enters the mortal world
Wake me up
When spring comes again
Wake me up
When the cold season ends
Wake me up
When the mercury rises
And the sun starts shining again

You can't convince me
You fell out of love with me
After one argument
You fell out of love with me
Just because I told you
That you hurt me
Were you threatened by what I said?
Or by how you made me feel?
But what I think happened was
You never loved me
So, I need to leave
I should be with someone who loves me

When people tell me
Hades is cold and cruel
I like to remind them
Hades is my protector
He can be cold and cruel
That much is true
But only when he must be
Have we all forgotten
He let Orpheus and Eurydice go
He cares for all the dead
Loves Persephone with all his heart
He is anything but cold and cruel

Destiny is a fickle thing
It can turn at any moment
Your life can change
In the blink of an eye
It can be scary
But it can be interesting and exciting
It all depends on where you stand

Goddess knows I want you
But you don't want me
Is what I keep telling myself
Because I am too scared to ask
Because the distance is too much
Because I don't want to ruin
Our friendship, our connection
So, I choose to be your friend
Because I need you in my life

Do you think if we lived
In the same part of the world
We would find each other
Do you think if we lived
In the same part of the world
We would be together
I guess we'll never know
But I'd like to imagine we would
Because you live there
And I live here

If he doesn't respond to your message
He doesn't love you
If he doesn't tolerate
For you to have a different opinion
He doesn't love you
When he doesn't keep his promises
He doesn't love you
When you want to delete your profile
From the dating app you met
And you see he changed his profile picture
He doesn't love you
Even if he says he does

When people
Try to lecture me
On my Gods and Goddesses
I like to remind them
That I am descendant of a Goddess
With fire in my veins
They should not speak of things
They don't understand

Real apologies
Are followed by changed behaviour
Instead of more of the same
Real apologies
Are followed by genuine remorse
Real apologies
Are not telling me my feelings are wrong

Shout out to whoever
Takes care of my name
When I am not in the room
Thank you for that
Know that I will do the same
For me, you are a true friend
Thank you for defending me
Even when I cannot hear you
Thank you for being there for me
Even when I am not around

I thought you'd be hot
Like the coffee we drank
But both you and the coffee
Were lukewarm
And that was quite disappointing

When I tell men I worship Athena
And she protects me
They bring false facts
I always get a bit angry
I do not like to be lectured on my gods
But Athena and me
We know why
This is what happens when insecure men
Are threatened by strong women
Athena and I are not afraid
She has dealt with such men before
And I dealt with you

I wanted you to grab my hand
To hold it and never let it go
I wanted to hug you
And never let you go
I just wanted you
But then I got to know you
And I realised
How we don't match
I am ambitious
You are happy where you are
I value movement
You are content sitting on the couch
I like honesty
And you haven't been honest with me
So, this could never work

You gave me something
And I lost it
And I feel terrible
Even though, I am incredibly sad
About losing your gift
I am miserable thinking how you
Now, think that I am careless
And that I don't care about you
Because I do I care about you
I want to make you happy, not sad
Because you are special to me
And I will do everything to make this right

I am alone
But never lonely
For I have my pen
And my paper
And my books
My longtime friends
My confidants
My lifelines

It is time to put on the armour
And get ready for war
This is what it feels like
To be around you
To have to see you
It feels like battle
Like a f*ucking war
But, sadly for you
I worship a war Goddess
She will help me take you down
Watch it, darling, me and Athena,
We are coming for you
And you will regret the day
You decided to hurt me
Today, we'll ride to battle
Today, we'll come home victorious

When I am happy
I tend to turn into a little child
I think it's because I feel
I had to grow up too fast
So, when I am upset
I tend to look for things
That give me the feeling
Of childlike wonder
So, I can forget
My sorrows and problems

I am like a phoenix
Because like the mythical bird
I, too, rise from the ashes
The remnants of the demons
That I fought and defeated
On my own
And occasionally
My demons rise from the ashes
But I always conquer them anew
I wrestle them into submission
I claw at their faces
I knock out their teeth
I fight them until there are no more

How can I be homesick
For a place that never has been my home
I shouldn't feel this way about a city
It feels like travelling gone wrong
I feel safe here, I feel at home
These famous landmarks
The giant eye, the towering clock
I love it here, my London
Someday, you will be my home

I am very lovable
Because I am funny and I'm strong
I am quirky and have pretty eyes
I am loyal and give great advice
I write you poems
And I love with all my heart

Somebody once told me
That making memories
Is the most important thing to do in life
So, I choose to do that
To visit more places
To do more things
To go to special events
To make new friends
And I am no longer afraid
Because I want all the memories I can get
Someday, I want to look back on my life
And see happiness and good life

You are my lighthouse
My beacon in my darkest night
My light to guide me
In the wildest storms
You are my home
My safe haven
My best friend
And I will protect you
Body, soul, and mind
With my life

You only knew my name
When you needed something from me
You only knew my name
When it benefited you
But I knew your name
Through it all, I stood by you
But my name died on your lips
Ignored, neglected, unspoken
I mistook convenience for love
So, this is my goodbye

My dear,
You made a poet fall in love with you
And now you are going to live forever
Everyone will know how you loved me
How your eyes look at me
How you smell and how your touch feels
Everyone will know you are my everything
My protector, my partner, my best friend
And everyone will know how I love you
How you are like a breath of fresh air
After years of inhaling smoke
How you are like a full moon
After decades without any light

# Acknowledgements

I am extremely grateful for Butterdragons Publishing, for taking this chance on me and guiding me on this journey. You have made my dreams come true and I will be eternally thankful for that.

I would like to express special gratitude to my English teachers. Mrs. Van Bennekum, thank you for always believing in me. Mr. Waddup, thank you for helping me overcome my eating disorder. I am eating now, sir, I promise. Mr. Paliama, thank you for always being honest with me. In the end, you were always right. The three of you have formed my English. Thank you.

I would also like to thank my bullies. I couldn't have done this without your persistent harassment. I may not have re-written a bestseller, as some of you mockingly said, I have my own book. I may forget, but I will never forgive. Look at me now!

Lastly, I would like to thank my parents, my grandparents, and my best friend. Thank you, for always supporting me, guiding me and believing in me

# About Fay van Burg

Fay is a Dutch poet and a fiction writer. She draws her inspiration from heart breaking moments and combines them with her everyday experiences. Her themes of interest are eclectic and vary from online dating to modern views on ancient myths. She writes it all! Fay also uses her voice to draw attention to mental health issues and raise awareness. She writes in hope her words will resonate with her readers and make them feel less alone and believe more in their own magic.

When she's not writing, Fay loves spending time with her lovely horse Shadow and her black cat Salem.

## Other BDP books by Fay van Burg

Fighting the Madness
Collection of Tragic Love Stories

9 789493 287730